You're Free**r**
than you think

by
Bob Duncan

to Ara
Besides myself, the
first to benefit from these
stories

CONTENTS

"Come to the edge, he said.
We are afraid, they said.
Come to the edge, he said.
They came to the edge,
He pushed them and they flew.
Come to the edge, Life said.
They said: We are afraid.
Come to the edge, Life said.
They came. It pushed them...
And they flew."

—Guilliame Apollinaire

INTRODUCTION

When circus elephants are young, a shackle is placed around their leg to keep them in one spot. Chained to a stake that's been driven into the ground, they learn that it's impossible to escape because they're too weak. Later, as adults, they have more than enough strength to free themselves but no longer try because the belief they acquired when they were young still controls them. Sound familiar?

Like everyone else, I was born into the limitations of our race consciousness. Everything in my life has been played out according to the parameters defined by those beliefs. I have been a walking, talking set of beliefs; beliefs I acquired from my family, friends, the media, etc.

Years ago, I temporarily unshackled myself from that programming. No longer grounded, I was able to jump off cliffs from the known into the unknown over and again, always landing on my feet. I was able to accomplish things that had formerly seemed impossible. I experienced the parting of the Red Sea of negative programming long enough to see that the limitations I'd believed in were false. The struggle I'd been playing out was a delusion; a direct result of the thoughts and ideas I'd accepted as true. And I just thought I'd been dealt a lousy hand in life.

I first heard of the law of attraction in 1988 after buying a cassette tape called Prosperity. It was a guided meditation that encouraged the listener to envision what they wanted in life. I listened to it repeatedly for a time and did notice a shift in my consciousness; for instance, my relationship with money.

1

When I had no problem giving a tip to a taxi driver, I realized something had changed because I'd usually felt a sense of loss when spending money. The underlying anxiety that there wasn't enough had been replaced with a feeling of abundance.

Unfortunately, with time, I eventually stopped listening to the tape and defaulted back to my unchecked belief system. The cold, hard facts of life took over my thoughts once again. I refer to them as "cold, hard facts" because I'd grown convinced that life was an uphill battle and that thinking otherwise was a fantasy.

Consider the possibility that whatever situation you've been stuck in is actually a delusion, no matter how hopeless it may appear. The following accounts were the first times I had the guts or craziness to do the next right thing despite what the committee in my head told me would happen. In so doing, I went through a rabbit hole that I didn't even know was there and discovered that there really were solutions to my so called "insoluble" problems.

There's no accident that you're reading this. Whoever you are – greetings to you from another human being who is reminding you or perhaps telling you for the first time, "You're freer than you think."

From Greece to Paris

In 1978, I was twenty-five years old and living in a small apartment on 8th Street in New York City. I had wanted to live in Manhattan for years because I thought the right place and the right things would make me happy. I loved New York, but living there (or any place else) wasn't giving meaning to my life.

I was as lost as the piece of puzzle that had never seen the front of the box. Each day was the next spin of a turning hamster wheel. After enough turns, questions began to burn inside of me; "Is there a God?" and "Why am I here?"

When I couldn't take any more of it, I decided to start over again by leaving the country and venturing into the unknown. I had to find out the answers to a lot of things. Anything was better than unconsciously rotating another 365 spins around the wheel again.

About this time, I had also taken up photography. Until then my experience with cameras had been limited, but since I was turning a new page, I went out and bought a 35mm camera. Just as an unexamined dream has been called "an unopened letter to yourself", in hindsight I can see how photographs reflected not only where I was, but in some cases, where I was going. I understand now why Einstein said, "Imagination is more powerful than knowledge."

At the time, I was working at Windows on the World – the restaurant located on the 107th floor of the former World Trade

Center. It was there that I made friends with the receptionist, Cristine, who happened to be French.

I was practicing studio portraiture, and asked her to be one of my subjects. During the shoot I told her of my plan to go to Europe. Unexpectedly, she offered to arrange for me to stay with her sister for the first two weeks. She stipulated that after that, it would be up to me. From my current vantage point, I can see that my "intention" had manifested a very necessary component: the starting point for my journey. Paris.

A few weeks later I also asked my friend Susan to sit for me. Her great sense of humor started the session off with a lot of laughs. Photographically it wasn't going anywhere, but our discussion got interesting when it turned to philosophy and spirituality. I mentioned that I felt lost and was about to set out on an adventure in an attempt to find some answers. When she asked me if I believed in God, I told her I thought of myself as an agnostic; she said she was a believer.

I kept clicking away at the shutter while considering what she'd said. Then it occurred to me to ask her to imagine looking into the face of God. An idea of how to pose her came to me. I saw a marble bust of a 17th century French nobleman wearing a huge wig of curls with fabric swathed around the shoulders. I decided to go with it and asked her to untie her ponytail. She bent over and tousled her hair. When she looked up, a mass of waves framed her face. Then, to recreate the fabric, I took a sheet and draped it around her.

When I peered through the lens I was struck by the utter calm her face had taken on. With film, you never knew if what you'd seen had been captured or not until you saw the print. When I did see the result, that fulfilled look that had haunted me was still there. Her inner peace was some part of the "fixed point" I was searching for.

Looking at her gaze brought to mind words I'd heard in a program I'd just watched about Howard Carter's discovery of King Tut's tomb. It was a tribute written for the young pharaoh:

May you spend millions of years
You who love Thebes
Sitting with your face
To the north wind
Your two eyes
Beholding happiness

In only a few months, I found myself with my apartment subleased, my job terminated, and many farewells said and done. Then an unexpected emergency emptied my nest egg. I was left with forty-three dollars. It seemed simple logic that I could no longer go to Europe since I needed money. The lack of money had always limited me. My whole life I'd been encased in the belief that without money I couldn't do anything. I was so fed up with one step forward, two steps back, on the day of the flight departure I threw caution to the wind and boarded the plane. I figured that if there was something out there that could help me, I needed to find out about it sooner than later.

I remember seeing in an old Tarzan movie, a wobbly rope bridge that spanned a deep chasm. The protagonists hurriedly made their way across as the jungle drums grew louder. They were advised not to look down for fear of losing their nerve. When they got to the opposite side, Tarzan cut the rope and the bridge collapsed behind them. Precarious as it looked, I would've preferred crossing that rope bridge to boarding the plane with only chump change in my pocket because I had nothing to grab onto but thin air and faith.

In Paris, Cristine's sister, Sylvie, put up a notice where she worked announcing that I was available to paint apartments. Someone hired me and I began generating a small income. I can't remember all the "connecting of the dots" that kept sustaining me, but I was steadily aware that I hadn't fallen through the net. At the time, I wrote it off as "luck".

Paris exceeded my expectations. Aesthetic beauty surrounded me at every turn which made it impossible not to try to capture it on film.

But the only adventuring I was doing was through my camera. I knew I was leveling off. I had to keep moving. I'd fallen into a comfort zone and my greater purpose of discovering God and the meaning of life had gone dormant. Paris had been the starting point, but I needed to know where to go next because I didn't know what I was doing. I needed something to inspire me anew.

In France, most building light switches are on timers. Right after leaving a friend's place, before switching on the hallway light, I noticed the afternoon sun streaming through the slit of space by a door that had been left ajar.

For a moment its porcelain knob was set off dramatically with rays of light emanating from it. I took out my camera and clicked the shutter.

It would be more than a year before I'd have the money to develop my film, but I couldn't forget the image of that unlocked doorway in the darkness beckoning me. I didn't realize then that it was a portent of what was to come.

After a year in Paris, I had the urge to see more of Europe and decided to move to Amsterdam. Once there, I got a job as a dish washer in a small café; my only task was to load the machine and turn the knob! One night, I met a couple who asked what I was doing living abroad. I told them I was pretty much going wherever the wind blew me. They mentioned they owned a farm in Greece and were about to make a trip down there, and that if I was interested in joining them, to meet them in Frankfurt the following Thursday. If I didn't show up it was all the same to them. Thinking it was a great opportunity to venture off in a completely new direction, I gladly accepted their offer.

The next Thursday my hosts and I packed up their Volkswagen van and we set our course south. Our first stop was a small village in Austria where we stayed with a family overnight.

In the dining room of their friend's home yet another image of light caught my attention. One of the glass doors separating the room had transformed the blank light on one side into a defined shape on the other. I didn't know why it intrigued me so much; perhaps because I myself was undergoing a transition?

The next day we crossed the border into Yugoslavia, but because of a blizzard, all I got to see of it was the occasional outline of a building or the carcass of an abandoned vehicle along the highway. We drove straight through the whole length of the country, and sometime the following night we arrived at their farm in Greece. When the headlights went out, I saw the night sky blaze with more stars than I'd ever seen before. We were far away from everything.

At first, I considered living on a farm next to the Mediterranean more of my great journey into the unknown. But I had no money, so I offered to do work in exchange for my keep. That changed my status from adventurer to indentured servant. I discovered over time that this was why I had been invited. Things soured quickly after that.

Something changed with my hosts. Within months, they stopped speaking English and became nothing more than silent figures. They would occasionally emerge from their shuttered house and move about the grounds attending to various tasks, then vanish. I was left entirely alone; no more conversation; no more laughter.

The monotony was mind numbing. There was no phone, television, or radio; in fact, no distractions of any kind. The Chinese water torture of dead silence every hour of every day went on relentlessly until it was pounding in my head. There were times when I couldn't take another minute of it and I'd go out in the field and yell as loud as I could. Sometimes I'd yell until I was hoarse, but the moment I stopped, the silence would close back in on me. In the meantime, the work continued to accumulate. One day I found myself sitting among buckets of bloody chickens, plucking the feathers out one by one, knowing there'd be no end to it. I was trapped and had no one to turn to.

One evening, a storm broke out. The noise caused by the rustling tree branches convinced me that a snake or rat was making its way into my room. Unable to sleep, I lay in bed and stared at the ceiling while listening to the endless barking of their dog. I went to the window and stared out into the night.

As I watched the trees bending in the wind and rain, I began to wonder where everything came from. It was the same kind of curiosity I'd had as a kid when I questioned where God came from. Noticing my hands resting on the window ledge, I wondered where I came from. Then, almost imperceptibly, a kind of knowingness overtook me. It became as strong as a conviction: the idea that I was free to go anytime I wanted to.

Dr. Wayne Dyer once told an audience that even when he was confronted with evidence given to him by doctors proving that he had leukemia, he declared within himself that he was whole and healthy. He ignored "the proof" and through a determination to heal, ultimately found himself in full remission. He urged the audience to ignore the "evidence" their senses tell them and to follow their inner vision instead.

A similar kind of attitude overtook me. Despite overwhelming odds, I suddenly knew, without a shadow of a doubt, that I was free. I didn't know who or what I was talking to, but I said out loud that I knew I could get to Paris in two days.

I didn't realize it then, but it was the first time I had used my mind to visualize an end result. I sensed that something greater than I was allowing me to see that I had the power to actualize realities created by my thoughts. Like a child taking my first unassisted steps I was discovering that my ability to manifest what I wanted had been dormant within me all along. I was no longer a victim of circumstances. Suddenly feeling empowered, I made the decision to leave for Paris the next day.

"I have learned silence from the talkative,
Toleration from the intolerant, and
Kindness from the unkind; yet strange,
I am ungrateful to these teachers."

~ Kahlil Gibran

The day after a storm is always beautiful, but the next morning had a freshness unlike any other. When my hosts left for the local village to get supplies, I watched their van drive off into the distance until they were finally out of sight, then headed back to my room. I had a lot of things with me, but packed only a small suitcase. I took one last look at the farm and silently said goodbye to it and its owners. In time, I became grateful to them for helping to forge the circumstances which had enabled me to make the most important discovery of my young life. With my bag and a German ten-mark note, I started out for Paris on foot.

At first, I ran as fast as I could to gain distance. I would run, catch my breath, and then run again. Finally, when I felt sure they wouldn't find me, I slowed to a walk. The more distance I gained, the more intoxicated I became with the rush of being free again. I didn't care if I had to sleep on the gravel and eat the roots from weeds. I was free!

After walking for hours, I saw some farm workers waiting for a bus; the first new faces I'd seen in months. I sat down to wait with them, still exhilarated by the experience of being out in the world again. Then it occurred to me that I didn't have the right currency for the bus fare. I showed my German mark and pointed to the pavement but no one responded.

I saw an old man with a donkey making his way toward us. When he got nearer, I approached him too. I walked out to the highway and drew the outline of a bus and flashed my money. He didn't speak but reached into his pocket and handed me a coin; the exact fare needed for the bus!

I thanked him and he continued to make his way down the road. Something remarkable had just happened. Moments earlier, I didn't have bus fare. Then, this old man materialized and handed it to me. Coincidence? Maybe.

The bus route ended at a juncture in the road. Two buildings stood opposite each other; one was a tavern, the other a general store. My instinct told me to go into the store and change my marks for drachmas, but when I looked at the old peasant woman behind the register, I hesitated. What would she want with German currency out here? But the idea persisted until I acted on it.

I went up to her and gestured that I needed my money converted. She didn't like the idea. Normally I would've been discouraged because she complained so much, but I calmly asked her again. Then something broke her resistance and I saw her bang open the register, take my note, and count it back to me in drachma. I had the odd sensation that I'd glimpsed five minutes into the future, because somehow I'd known it was going to happen that way.

Just as I left her, I saw another woman outside with a suitcase waiting for a bus. I had no idea where the bus was going or even if I had enough for the fare, but it was clearly the next thing to do. When the driver pulled up, I climbed aboard and with both my hands in front of me, I held out all the money the old woman had given me. Amused, he picked out the amount for the fare. I walked to the back of the bus, took a seat, and off we went.

As soon as I got comfortable in my seat I fell asleep. I didn't wake up until later that night when we came to the final stop: Thessaloniki. As I filed out with the other passengers, I wondered where to go next. Because I had so little money, I headed for the nearby park so I could find a place to sleep. For food, I hoped to find leftovers behind some restaurant.

Then the inner calm that had guided me all day put a very impractical idea into my head. The idea: to spend all my remaining money on a hotel room. I struggled with that. Why would I throw away what little I had on just one night's stay? The argument came back that I needed a comfortable bed and a good night's sleep. I thought it was crazy and kept trying to ignore it but it wouldn't go away. Finally I gave in and said, "Okay, okay, I'll go to a hotel!"

I approached several places. Each time I showed my money I'd see the same disappointing shake of the head. More than once I was walked out to the street where someone would point far down the road and say, "Olympia". My feet were so tender I felt I couldn't take another step, but after hearing it a third time, I began reluctantly trudging toward the Olympia.

Along the way I passed a travel agency. It had a window display with a cardboard cutout of Europe. A one-way arrow pointed from Greece to London's Big Ben. Beside the arrow was the number sixteen-hundred. The number was the only thing I could recognize. To pass the time I tried guessing the approximate exchange rate of sixteen-hundred drachma to dollars.

At last I arrived at the Olympia. They accepted my money and even handed me back a few coins. Even though I'd just spent everything I had, I remained calm as the attendant led me to my room. The whole day had gone as smooth as silk.

After showing me to my room, the attendant left and closed the door behind him. The sound of the door closing shut was like hearing the snap of fingers and the words, wake up. I came out of my hypnotic spell and looked around. It suddenly hit me that I had wandered hundreds of miles off course and had spent all of my money!

I immediately felt like a drowning man flailing in the water. I was wild with fear. The idea of calling my parents for a wire transfer raced through my head. In a panic, I got on the phone to place an international call. When the operator came on I strained to make out what she was saying in the wavering static. She said the number didn't answer but that she'd call me back when she'd made a connection. When I hung up I tried to reassure myself that it would all be okay. Too anxious to sit and wait, I decided to take a shower.

With the water running, I heard the phone ring and ran to answer it. The operator explained that the number in the U.S. didn't answer and offered to keep trying. I don't know why, but I said, "That's okay, cancel the call," and put the receiver down. I sat on the bed with the phone in my lap and stared at the sliding glass doors to the balcony. What made me cancel the call?

I went over the day in my head. I remembered the wonder I had felt when the old man, who seemingly came out of nowhere, handed me bus fare. From that point I had simply watched as one door opened onto another. I'd instinctively known what to do, step by step.

Looking back through the years, I recognized that doors had always been opening for me. The more I considered, the more my state of mind shifted from feeling desperate to wanting to express gratitude. I didn't know where I had come from, or what this mysterious life was all about, but I wanted to give something back to whatever cause and effect had put everything into existence including me.

I got down next to the side of the bed and closed my eyes. With my mind, I created a gift. I began to imagine an image of light; something like a vertical aurora borealis. Suspended somewhere out in space, it was so vast a galaxy of stars surrounded it. I became aware that it was me that was creating it and not even God had seen it before. The fear and anxiety began to lessen as I held the vision uninterrupted for several minutes. Finally I opened my eyes. To the best of my ability, I'd given thanks for a lifetime of blessed moments.

Although I was worn-out and hungry, I wasn't ready for bed so I decided to take a short walk before retiring. Just as I was leaving the hotel, directly across the street from me, I saw something that left me dumbstruck. It was a shop that bought and sold used cameras, the only thing I had of value with me.

The timing and positioning were astonishing. It felt as if it had been staged just for me. In sci-fi TV shows, when someone steps into a time warp the screen image wavers like the surface of water to represent the entry into a mysterious portal in time and space. Right after seeing the shop, each proceeding moment felt unfamiliar; like I'd stepped into another dimension. I walked across the street and approached the owner. He just happened to speak English; not even the hotel staff spoke English. I asked if he was interested in the model of camera I had. When he said he was, I was beside myself and raced back to my room to get it.

Before returning, I paused… I realized I didn't know the exchange rate of Greek currency and was about to negotiate with a merchant. Then the figure from that travel agency floated back into my head. I didn't know how much it was, but it was the only reference I had. When he asked me the price, I took a chance with it and said, "sixteen-hundred." Just like the old peasant woman earlier in the day, at first he scoffed. He countered, "fourteen-hundred." I listened to the counsel inside myself and just keep repeating "sixteen-hundred" each time he made a counteroffer. Then, just like the old woman, something broke his resistance and I watched as cash was being counted out into my hand.

The dictionary partly defines a miracle as something that happens when you need it to happen. This happened when I needed it to happen. With the money in my hand, I walked out onto the street, still in disbelief. I looked up at the balcony to my room where I'd been only 20 minutes earlier, paralyzed with fear. It all felt so strangely unreal that I half expected to turn around and see that the shop and its owner had disappeared like some Twilight Zone episode. As if playing back a video, I looked at the panic that had gone through me right after the attendant had left the room; how the voices inside of my head had scolded me for wandering off on a fool's errand. The same voices that had always told me everything I'd ever believed in. It was the first time I was displaced from them long enough to really see that I'd been in a kind of trance all my life. Somehow I'd gone through a looking glass into another reality, unaligned with those old beliefs.

"More and more people are reaching a point
where they have become capable of breaking
out of the inherited, collective mind patterns
that have kept humans in bondage
to suffering for eons."

~ Daniel Rechnitzer
The All Knowing Diary

I reviewed the day's events: first the coin, then the woman next to the suitcase, followed by the crazy idea of spending all my remaining money on a hotel room, the various people who directed me to the Olympia, coming upon the sign with the number sixteen-hundred, the coincidence that the Olympia happened to be the only hotel located directly across the street from a shop that was in the business of purchasing the only thing I had of value, and now all this money in my hand! I wanted everyone I'd ever known to feel the rush of what I was experiencing. I'd just overcome fantastic odds; but how? For a moment in time, the so called "logical" facts that had kept me imprisoned all my life were proven false. I had started out with no money, and yet because I kept heading in the right direction, the money manifested but I would never have known that if I hadn't taken the first step. It made me realize how many times I'd been quite close to the solution to a problem but had been too unaware to see it. I had always guided my life by what I could see in front of me, rather than the inner vision that could have created what I wanted. I had adopted the same belief system that had been standard for twenty centuries: there's not enough money, there's not enough time, there's not enough love, etc. But I had discovered a chink in the armor.

Back at the hotel, I had a hot meal just before the café closed. When I returned to my room, I rolled up the cash and stuffed it into one of my shoes in the closet.

The next morning found me not sleeping in the park or scrounging for food, but safe and well rested. Opening the closet and seeing the wad of money still in my shoe proved that I hadn't been dreaming.

I remember in Charles Dickens's "A Christmas Carol" how Ebenezer Scrooge awakened to a new life after his eventful night of revelations. He was so giddy he could hardly contain himself. The world had been bathed in new clarity and ironically the reality that greeted him was more substantial than the one he'd relinquished. The air was filled with promise and had a sweetness about it that permeated everything.

I'll never again know anything like that morning. It was like waking up within a dream. The night before had happened just as I'd remembered it: the panic and sense of hopelessness followed by a seismic change that shook my old beliefs to the ground. I remember how my heart leapt with joy over and again at the fact that it had really happened.

I headed straight for the train station and bought a ticket. That night I arrived in Paris. Before falling asleep, I looked up at the same moon I'd seen over a thousand miles away from the shack in Greece only two nights earlier. I'd said out loud to someone or something while I was still there, "If you can do all this, then you can get me to Paris in two days."

I'd heard it all my life, but it really was true; the answers were inside of me. I had been given a mind that could create thoughts of intention more powerful than I dared dream, and an inner map system run by intuition.

On a YouTube video I watched, a woman related the amazing account of a man who'd escaped Auschwitz because he wasn't willing to accept that there wasn't a way out. One day while witnessing the bodies from the gas chambers being loaded onto trucks and driven out of the gates, the solution came to him.

The following day he undressed and threw himself among the corpses, pretending to be dead. His body was loaded onto the truck along with the others and he was transported to a distant location. The truck stopped at an open grave and he was thrown into the pit with the risk of being buried alive. At an opportune moment, he climbed out and escaped into the forest.

Each time I've learned of situations in which people broke past supposedly impossible barriers it reaffirms my belief that there are always solutions, even when there appear to be none.

Sadly, even though I'd just undergone an astonishing experience which defied fantastic odds, in time I returned to my old way of thinking. With the whole world supporting the idea of lack and limitation, it wasn't hard to fall into the rhythm of it again. I didn't recognize my part in it until it occurred a second time. It took a house falling on me to realize how free I was, but as is often said, "It takes what it takes."

In a New York Minute

"As a single footstep will not make a path on the earth, so a single thought will not make a pathway in the mind. To make a deep physical path, we walk again and again. To make a deep mental path, we must think over and over the kind of thoughts we wish to dominate our lives."

~ Henry David Thoreau

Ten years later, while living in California, I received a job offer back in New York. I was reluctant to return at first, but the money was tempting so I agreed to their three month trial offer. Not wanting to settle into an apartment until I was certain, I made arrangements to stay at a residency hotel.

By summer's end I'd made my decision to return to LA. Then, shortly after cashing my last paycheck, my wallet went missing. I found myself not only completely broke, but with no identification. The modest room I was renting featured a bare light bulb in the ceiling, a sink in the corner, and a twin bed. In two days I'd be without it, too.

I thought of registering with a temporary agency to earn some quick cash. Even though I was qualified for a number of positions, without identification I was turned away. I tried to keep a clear perspective but fear got the best of me. In 48 hours I'd have no place to live. I pressed an old panic button and decided to call my dad for help.

Earlier in June, I'd called him for Father's Day. For whatever reason, I'd chosen that day of all days to express resentments I'd held in for years. In a matter of fact voice, I included the fact that since I'd left home he'd never once picked up the phone and called me.

In 1988 the sound of static during long distance calls sounded something like a seashell held next to your ear. I listened to it as I waited for his response. He finally spoke. Surprisingly, he sounded pleased, and acknowledged that I'd said things I had every right to say. It felt good to have earned his respect, but now here I was calling him in a very different frame of mind. I knew that if I asked him for money, I'd be throwing away everything I'd gained, but fear kept me putting one foot in front of the other until I reached the phone booth.

When he answered, I could hear by the sound of his voice that he was pleased to hear from me. We chatted for a while about this and that. Then, after stalling as long as possible, I said, "Oh, by the way..." I could feel the energy shift and when he finally did speak, all the warmth I'd heard before was gone. He asked, "What is it?" I told him I needed help and offered empty promises to repay him. An uncomfortable silence followed as I cowered back into the shadows. I knew he had no money himself. Finally, he replied, "Well son, this is the bottom of the barrel." That was hard to hear, but harder still was the next line. "And you will have to pay me back." He said he'd overnight the money and ended the call abruptly. All the life inside of me drained away as I put the receiver down.

Back in my room, I went over to the bed and sat down. When I turned off the overhead light, the only thing that offered visual relief was the nightly display that occurred at the window.

24

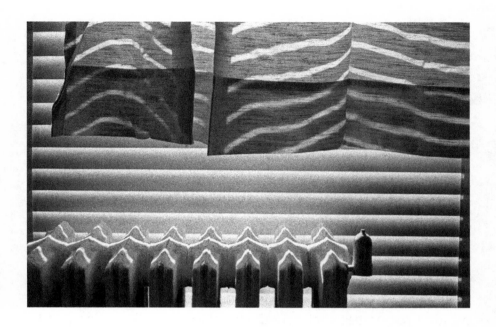

Each evening, the light from the street would glow through the venetian blinds and float in waves on the piece of curtain that hung just above the chevrons of the radiator.

I looked back through the years. I'd attended seminars, human potential movement programs, listened to motivational speakers, undergone encounter groups, taken up individual therapy, group therapy, and on and on, all in an effort to rewire myself. But here I was, once again, stone broke. I was baffled by it all. In Greece I'd been liberated, and for a moment in time had known that I was free; yet here I was imprisoned again.

It's funny how random thoughts come to mind at the oddest moments. A scene from a Planet of the Apes movie popped into my head. The gorillas had heard about what had formerly been Manhattan, and were marching on it to attack its remaining human residents. The inhabitants' only defense was the ability to place mental images into the thoughts of lesser beings. They projected an apparition into the minds of the gorillas; an image of a huge statue of their ape god standing amid a great wall of fire. When the phantom image appeared the cavalry retreated in fear, but the leader shrewdly recognized that the fiery specter was an illusion. He yelled out to the army, "This is false!" and the bleeding colossus, engulfed in flames, vanished. I looked around the room. Even though my senses told me that what was in front of me was real, my heart told me something else.

I began looking at the limiting beliefs I held and the concepts I'd been raised with like, "We can't afford that," or "A penny saved is a penny earned. Work hard and one day when you've saved enough you can..." Then Greece came to mind. I remembered clearly the exhilaration of knowing that I was freer than I'd ever imagined. Yet even though I had learned it, the "hard facts of life" had taken over my thinking anyway and left me once again feeling flightless and grounded. If I had the power to create then why had I experienced such suffering and impoverishment? Then I saw it. I had been creating. I'd created every circumstance that ensured that I would stay exactly where I was. It wasn't "God's will" – it was my will. What I did with my thoughts determined my destiny. With new clarity, I saw that the circumstances I found myself in were only reflections of my consciousness. If that were true, then I could change them.

With that, I sat down and began to write a letter to my dad telling him the money wasn't necessary. With each word I wrote, I felt stronger. I imagined myself in a prosperous setting with all my needs met. I saw myself in luxurious surroundings, happy and content. All the things I'd set forth with him months earlier came back, along with the esteem I'd earned from him.

By the end of the letter, I was renewed. I promised myself that when I received the money order the next morning I would take it to the bank, transfer it to his name, and mail it back. I was willing to live in the park in a refrigerator box and face myself square on rather than live begging for money. What was my father's was his and what was mine was mine. If I hadn't manifested it, it wasn't his fault. I went to sleep that night full of hope. If the limiting beliefs that had kept me in Greece could be proven false, then the ones I was harboring now could be too.

Each room in the hotel had what looked like a smoke alarm above the door, although it was actually a buzzer. If a package arrived, the buzzer would sound and scare the life out of you. The next morning, it suddenly went off. Knowing it meant my father's package had arrived, I headed out toward the lobby. The desk clerk had me sign for it. The moment I was holding it in my hands, I began to have second thoughts. I was very hungry and began reasoning that although my ideals had seemed noble last night, in the light of day, they seemed completely unrealistic, if not crazy. I tried focusing on the sense of peace that had overtaken me while writing the letter. I waffled back and forth. I did everything I could to revive the memory of Greece to Paris. Once again I thought about how good I'd felt the night before while writing the letter to my dad. I returned to my room, got the letter, and started for the bank.

With every step I took, the argument intensified. On the one hand, I thought, I was in charge of taking care of myself and there was no shame in asking for help; on the other was my memory of Greece. I didn't know if I had it in me to perform another trapeze act of faith like setting out for Paris on foot. That was then, this was now.

When I reached the bank, I stepped into the line of people making their way through the roped off area. It was all I could do to keep walking up to the next position each time someone moved ahead. Every second that I held onto my crazy idea was a test of will. I kept reliving the feeling I'd had while writing the letter to keep the doubt from tormenting me.

At last I got to the teller. I blurted out what I'd rehearsed, for fear I'd lose my nerve. She took the money order and slid back a new, blank one. I filled in my father's name and along with the letter placed the check in the envelope and stepped outside.

Urgently I searched for a mailbox. As soon as I spotted one, and before I lost my nerve, I opened the slot and dropped it in. The moment I saw the envelope disappear down the chute, I went into paralyzing shock. My beliefs began to assault me, telling me it was the beginning of the end and that tomorrow night I would be homeless.

While heading back to the hotel, my senses were so numb I bumped into a pedestrian more than once. I felt like I was trying to walk across the bottom of a deep swimming pool.

When I got close to the hotel, I went into the deli next door. With my remaining eighty cents I bought a half loaf of bread.

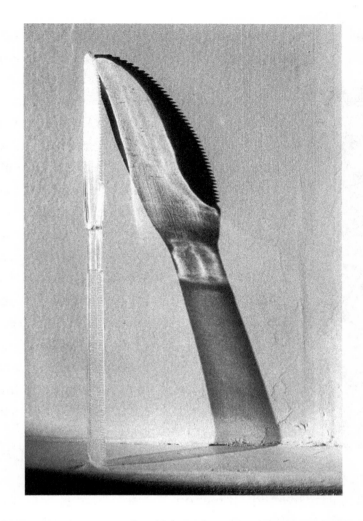

Back in my room I ate all of it, and washed it down with water from the tap. Once finished, I took in the realization that there was no more money for anything. I had reached the end of the line.

I leaned a plastic picnic knife against the wall and wondered when or where I would eat next.

I couldn't face any more. Even though the sheets were on fire from the sun, I didn't care. I just wanted to go to sleep and never wake up again.

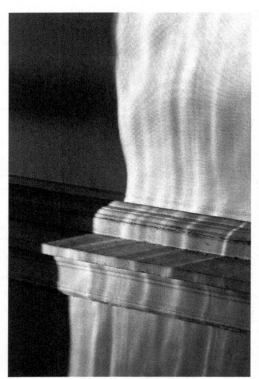

I lay on my side with the heat beating down on me and stared blankly at the pattern of light on the wall until I dropped off.

I slept for most of the day and woke up around five o'clock, wringing wet. More time had passed and I was that much closer to being out on the street. The only thing I could think of was what a crazy thing I'd done and that I'd completely lost all sense of reason.

A few months back I'd come across a notice for a Debtors Anonymous meeting held at St. Vincent's Hospital. It met on Thursday nights, and it just happened to be a Thursday night that found me on the edge of homelessness. It crossed my mind that if I told someone in the group what I'd done, they might tell me that I'd acted on the right principle and hadn't gone over the edge. I needed someone to reassure me that I'd done the right thing. That's all I wanted to know.

I had arrived a bit late so the meeting was already in progress. It turned out to be a group of business owners. Seated around a large conference table were seven people. I pulled out a chair and sat down. They were talking about the financial condition of each of their businesses. I felt out of place. They all seemed so busy and important compared to me.

When everyone else had spoken, the leader asked if I wanted to say anything. I related my circumstances and explained that I believed we were each entitled to our own prosperity and shouldn't have to borrow it from others. Then I told them that I'd just mailed back a loan from my father, based on that premise.

In a 12-step meeting, when someone has finished speaking it's not customary to share comments or give feedback. Because of this, everyone remained silent after I spoke. I began feeling self-conscious. Realizing I'd just revealed the craziness of my thinking, I immediately left when the meeting ended. I was halfway down the block when I heard a man calling after me. I stopped to let him catch up. A bit out of breath, he smiled and asked, "Did you really send the money back to your father that way?" I told him that I had. He then said that he wasn't absolutely certain as he had to run the idea past his business partner first, but he believed he could help me. He wrote down his name and an address, and asked me to meet him there tomorrow if I had nothing better to do. Not only did his voice sound genuine, the look in his eyes gave me hope.

All that night, as well as the next morning, I tried to imagine what form of "help" he might offer. I thought he may be the owner of an apartment building. I pictured him taking me to a basement door. After opening it, he'd feel around for the pull chain to a light. When the light bulb came on, I'd see a cot next to a heater. Maybe he was going to offer it to me as a place to stay. That would be a miracle, but I tried not to expect

31

too much. I just knew that I really didn't want to sleep out in the open.

The next day I arrived at the address. It was a luxury high-rise. Confused, I walked up to the doorman and told him I was there to meet a guy named Mike. He escorted me to the lobby where I sat on the edge of a sofa and waited. Finally Mike arrived. I could see he'd come in with someone else. The doorman lit up when they walked in and gestured over to me. Mike came up and shook my hand, then introduced me to his business partner, Joe.

Their positive spirits felt like the sun when it first hits your eyes after emerging from a darkened movie theater. It hurt to "pretend" to be cheerful. I just wanted to know what they were planning.

We took an elevator to the 16th floor and I followed them to the door of one of the apartments. Waiting in the hallway, I overhead them saying things like, "Not every room has cable TV, but most do." I had no idea what they were talking about.

When we were gathered in the living room I was still unclear as to what was going on. Looking straight at me, Mike said, "Well, we don't know you from Adam, but here they are," and held up a set of keys in front of me. I didn't understand. Keys to what? What was he talking about? I thought they'd mistaken me for someone looking to rent an apartment and reminded them that I didn't have any money. They both looked at my confusion.

Mike sat me down and began to explain, telling me a bit about himself. Up until a year ago, he'd been an angry man who stuffed down his feelings with food and had gained over a hundred pounds doing it. Then he'd discovered the twelve step program for food (OA) and over time, lost the weight that had made him so miserable. With each stage of healing he had become more aware that God was giving him back his life. "Believe me, I've never given anybody anything without expecting something back," he said, "but when I heard your story, I realized it was time for me to give something to someone just as God had done for me."

He went on to explain that he and Joe were brokers for condos. They leased them out to businesses that needed temporary residences for visiting executives. Since it was summer, a lot of places were vacant, and it seemed to them the perfect way to help me out. After Mike finished, Joe added that they thought they had a job for me as well, if I was interested. Then he handed me two twenties to buy food with.

Again, I was numb with shock, but of a completely different nature. It was the closest I'd ever gotten to the unexpected jolt I can only imagine people feel when they win the lottery. How could this be? People don't just hand over the keys to a luxury apartment to a perfect stranger, offer them a job, and then give them money, no strings attached. What should I think first? What should I do first?

In the story of Peter Pan, one day Peter unexpectedly reappears in Wendy's adult life. Encouraging her to fly again, she discovers that her ability to believe in magic had died with the passing years. When Mike handed me those keys, my forgotten faith became rekindled. Once again I was twenty-five and on that open highway in Greece, exhilarated by the world before me. It was the second time in my life I'd acted on an instinct that was urging me in a direction that my rational mind said was impossible.

The night before, while writing the letter to my father, I had visualized myself as safe and wanting for nothing. I'd believed with all my heart that it was a true fact that we were all entitled to prosperity. I reinforced that belief by taking the action of returning the money. It went against all reasonable logic. Yet once again I'd found my way back through that unlocked door, and everything that had told me I couldn't do it was proven false. I had created and acted upon a completely contrary thought pattern, one based solely on my inner vision. To my amazement, and for the second time, it had become real before my very eyes.

I returned to the residency hotel to check out. Having just come from a place where every luxury was at my disposal, when I reentered the room I could see the small mindedness and limitations I'd been living by all my life.

I'd spent the forty dollars Joe had given me for food, so I didn't have enough left for a taxi back uptown. But I didn't care; I'd walk uptown. I wasn't going to sleep in the park! Then I remembered that I needed to return a call from a friend. After finding a payphone, I explained that I was moving so I couldn't get together with him. He asked, "Do you want me to come by and give you a lift?" In all the years I'd formerly lived in Manhattan, I'd never met anyone who owned a car! He said he lived in Brooklyn now and had a station wagon, and that he'd be over soon.

Sure enough, shortly after, I watched his station wagon pull up. When he walked into my room he could hear the shouting of tenants down the hall. He asked diplomatically, "How long have you been here?" Little did he know that in a manner of speaking, it had been a lifetime, but I simply answered, "All summer."

While driving to the new address, he asked about the place. I just said, "Wait and see." When I unlocked the door and we walked in, I told him it was my apartment. I remember the look on his face as he kept repeating, "You're kidding, right?"

Over the next few months I went to work each day and collected a weekly paycheck. Piece by piece I restored all my identification. Now and then either Mike or Joe would call to alert me that the apartment I was living in had been rented, and they'd send me in a taxi to another building. I ended up living in luxurious apartments all over the upper eastside.

One night I had turned off all the lights where I lived, and while looking out at the skyline, a memory came to me. When I was twelve years old, I saw a movie with Frank Sinatra called Come Blow Your Horn. It was a comedy about a wealthy bachelor who lived in a swanky New York apartment, not unlike the one I was living in now. Watching it from our family car at the drive-in movies, I remember my parents asking, "How'd you like to live in that apartment?!" A childhood dream had been fulfilled. For a time, my home actually was a lavish New York penthouse!

The day came when I knew it was time to return to California. I walked into Mike and Joe's office and announced I was heading west. As soon as I finished my announcement, they both rose to their feet. Mike said, "Bob, know that any time you're in New York you have a job." Then Joe came up and shook my hand and handed me an envelope. A lot of emotions welled up inside of me. The whole experience had been like a spell of perfect weather.

In the elevator I opened the envelope. It contained a check for a hundred dollars, a going away present. Across the top they had written: Thanks – for the experience. They were thanking me! If I hadn't mailed that check back to my father I would have never met Mike and Joe, and may have never lived in comfort and safety or found a job. Once again, I saw how my limiting beliefs had been proven false. All I had done was the next right thing and yet I'd been liberated beyond my wildest dreams.

It takes either courage or insanity to step outside of the known world we believe in. To wobble across a tightrope with no net underneath is scary as hell. Why would anyone attempt it? It took these first two experiences for me to see past my own limiting beliefs. Twice I'd witnessed solutions to seemingly insoluble problems and twice I'd discovered the power of my thoughts. I'd simply been using them in the wrong way.

For a long time, prior to New York, I considered my trip from Greece to Paris a miracle from God. It was, but not in the way I had thought. I had believed that some outside force had parted the Red Sea for me and then went about its business. It wasn't until the second time around that I began to realize that the instruments that could free me were inherently in me. The miracle was that I'd been born with the ability to create my own reality. In fact, I had been creating my realities quite successfully for years. I had believed in poverty and limitation so powerfully I'd manifested it constantly.

What I discovered was that my subconscious mind was like a little child. Whatever I said it happily agreed with. If I said life was miserable, it would say, "Yes, life is miserable." If I said life is amazing, it would say, "Yes, life is amazing." It never occurred to me that if I changed my beliefs, I could change my life.

It's been said that when one person heals, they heal the whole lineage they're descended from. I had awakened from the spell my parents and their parents and their parents before them had been in. I freed myself long enough from the lies to see that there was a better way to live.

Onward and Upward

While writing this book, I got a call from a friend who asked if I would join him for coffee along with two of his friends who were moving to Barcelona. Since I'd lived there, he wondered if I might share some helpful tips with them. When I met them I asked what living arrangements they'd made. They said they had one night reserved in a hotel room. I asked where they were going to stay after that. They simply replied that they didn't know but would figure it out.

Sitting across from me were two people who were about to take a huge risk. Most would have thought it not just a risk, but just plain crazy. Nothing they were doing sounded plausible or realistic. They, like me, were starting off with little to no money. Yet something inside them had moved them toward the idea anyway. They had their one way tickets, just as I had had, and were willing to face whatever consequences awaited them. They just knew they were leaving and they were not going to let the lack of money stop them.

As they were departing in just a few weeks, we got together each Wednesday night and I shared with them as much as I could. I also sent a text to my friend Claudia, who lived in Barcelona, asking if she'd be available to meet them for coffee after they arrived. Our texting went back and forth before she told me that she'd lost her job and needed to downsize. Because she had a three bedroom place, she offered to rent one of the bedrooms to them for a low monthly fee. She felt it would be beneficial on both sides; she could use the extra rent money, and they needed a place to stay.

These two had no idea they'd meet me only weeks before their departure, and of course, I didn't know I'd meet them either, much less act as a go between for them. The very principle I wrote this book on was playing itself out in front of me. I took it to mean that I was doing the next right thing by writing about it.

While living in Barcelona, I saw this statue at the pinnacle of a building. It had a special significance for me because it symbolized the reemergence of life. The youth represents a new beginning, riding atop the mythical phoenix as it rises from the ashes of defeat. The old has to die in order for the new to emerge.

Keep the Faith

Most everyone has stories in which they can recount an unusual occurrence; someone calling at an unexpected but perfect moment, or just happening to be in the right place at the right time and things working out so well it left them wondering.

Until now I've kept these accounts to myself because they've simply been a way of life for me. But when I began to hear the buzz about the law of attraction, I recognized that I'd unknowingly been using it all along. I'm not a law-of-attraction expert and there are countless books and videos on the subject that explain how to enact it. All I know is that every time I've operated from a "law of attraction" awareness, the outcome has always left me stunned in amazement.

By following the innate guidance within me and having reassessed the power of my thoughts I've changed my life perspective completely. I have drawn upon these experiences time and again to give me the needed courage to face life's challenges. I can tell you that every time I've transfigured doubt into faith I've been lifted out of myself by an inexplicable *shift* in circumstances.

It is my sincere wish that you discover this facility within yourself... if you will only dare believe it.
Let me leave you with this:

"God has already blessed you with everything you need.
He can't bless you anymore."

~ Terry Cole-Whittaker

Recommended Reading:

Your Invisible Power
Genevieve Behrend

Mind Power into the 21st Century
John Kehoe

Manifest Your Destiny:
The Nine Spiritual Principles for Getting Everything You
Want
Dr. Wayne W. Dyer

It's Not about the Money
Bob Proctor

No Matter What
Lisa Nichols

Manifest Your Millions!
A Lottery Winner Shares his Law of Attraction Secrets
Eddie Coronado

The Magic of Believing
Claude M. Bristol